The Poor Immigrant
Who Became
Successful

The Poor Immigrant
Who Became
Successful

True Life Story

Harris Bobyigha Dobgima

ARPress
ILLUMINATING IDEAS
EMPOWERING VOICES

ARPress
45 Dan Road Suite 5
Canton MA 02021

Hotline: 1(888) 821-0229
Fax: 1(508) 545-7580

Ordering Information:

Quantity sales. Special discounts are available on quantity purchases by corporations, associations, and others. For details, contact the publisher at the address above.

Printed in the United States of America.

ISBN-13:   Paperback   979-8-89676-292-8
             eBook   979-8-89676-293-5

Library of Congress Control Number: 2025910434

Dedication

This book is dedicated to all those who have embarked on similar journeys, leaving behind everything they know in search of a better life. May your stories be heard and your struggles recognized.

Acknowledgment

Authoring this book has been a journey as remarkable as the one undertaken by our protagonist, and I owe a debt of gratitude to many who supported and inspired me along the way.

Primarily, I want to express my deepest gratitude to myself (Harris Bobyigha Dobgima), whose incredible story of resilience and courage is at the heart of this book.

To my family, thank you for your unwavering support and patience during the countless hours I spent immersed in writing. Your encouragement gave me the strength to persevere through the challenging moments.

I would like to extend my heartfelt thanks to my editor, whose insightful feedback and meticulous attention to detail helped shape this book into its final form. Your guidance has been invaluable.

Special thanks to Ndikum Claude for providing me with crucial information and insights into the cultural and historical context of Cameroon and the journey of African immigrants. Your expertise added depth and authenticity to the narrative.

To my friends and beta readers, your honest feedback and enthusiastic support kept me motivated and focused. I am grateful for your time and constructive criticism, which improved the manuscript.

I also wish to acknowledge the various organizations and individuals who assisted in my research. The stories and data shared by humanitarian groups, immigration services, and cultural experts were instrumental in providing a comprehensive understanding of the immigrant experience.

Finally, I want to thank my readers. Your interest and empathy for this story bring it to life and give it purpose. I hope this book serves as a reminder of the strength of the human spirit and the power of hope and determination. I want to thank every one of you for your invaluable contributions to my book. Your support, feedback, and encouragement have been instrumental in bringing this story to life.

Whether you shared your subjective experiences, provided expert advice, offered constructive criticism, or simply cheered me on, your involvement has made a significant impact. I am deeply grateful for your time, effort, and dedication.

Thank you for believing in this project and helping to make it a reality. Your contributions have enriched the narrative and added depth and authenticity to the story. I look forward to sharing the final product with you and the world.

With gratitude,
Harris Bobyigha Dobgima

X

HARRIS BOBYIGHA DOBGIMA
Information System Security Officer

Contact info:

potterharrio@yahoo.com(PayPal)

Tel: 442-270-1807 (Zelle)
Cashapp: $HarrisDobgima

Index

The hardships I faced during my journey to America could have easily gotten the worse of me. All the pain I encountered, whether physical, emotional, or mental, was hard to bear. I managed to get through it with the support of my family, wife, cousins, and unique and helpful people I met along my migration journey, especially with the Grace of God. I am about to unfold my journey with you guys, and after reading through it, you will learn how many people are willing to risk being in America. So, let's start my migration story, "MY TRIP TO THE UNITED STATE OF AMERICA."

My name is HARRIS; I am from CAMEROON (Northwest Region). There are six people in my family, i.e., my mum, dad, my brother, and my two sisters. I grew up in a poor household where we managed to get only two square meals a day. Things were very difficult for us to the point where I had to go to school and do odd jobs just to support my family and to meet my brother and sister's school needs and myself. I still glorify God because, despite all the hardship, we were still able to share with those who could barely have a meal per day. My younger brother had to quit school because my parents could not afford to send all of us to school, and the burden was too much on me.

My brother's sacrifice reduced my burden, and he had to look for a job to assist me. His decision to take up employment helped my family; we now had more earners. The condition became worse in 2009 when my dad got sick; his health deteriorated to the point that he had to undergo an operation on his belly. At that time, I took the challenge to quit school too, so that I could entirely focus on earning money. I had to work multiple jobs, such as selling food at my mum's restaurant and also riding a commercial motorcycle to assist my mum with the hospital bills, just so that she could pay for my dad's medications. Thank God!

Because the operation was successful, now my dad is strong, though not healthy, but the main thing is that he is alive and well.

After a couple of years, in 2011, my girlfriend passed away... It was a tragedy that I had never experienced. That tragic incident had a devastating impact on my mental health. The loss of a loved one surely drains all your happiness, and because of that, I gave up on the idea of l finding another girl. I was so displaced that it took me about five years to recover from that pain.

My cousin, who lived in Thailand, heard about what we were going through, and he decided to call my parents and chat with them about helping me travel to meet him in Thailand. In 2013, he did all my paperwork for me to join him in Thailand, and the biggest problem I encountered was how to raise money for my flight. I had to convince my parents to borrow money from the bank; they did so and gave it to me so that I could travel to Thailand.

I had to assure my parents that I would work hard to pay back the money and take care of them. They were also scared while all of this was happening, but along with me, it was my cousin who also convinced them to do so, and they eventually borrowed the money ($2000) and handed it to me.

My flight to Thailand went safely; on my arrival, my cousin and I started applying for jobs. Luckily, I got one for teaching after a couple of weeks. I moved from my cousin's residence and got accommodation at the place where the job was based. My salary was $500 a month. So, do the math; I earned $500 a month. I had to pay my bills, feed myself, take care of my family back home, and pay the debt I owed to the bank.

It is impossible to survive on such low pay, right? ...... Then, I had to travel to Malaysia for a visa change since I had arrived in Thailand with a tourist visa. My school assisted me with documentation to do the visa change since I was working for them, but before that could happen, I was working through an agency for three months, and the agent didn't pay me my salary. Every month, when I asked her about my salary, she said, "I gave your cousin your salary," on the other hand, she also told my cousin that she had given me my salary. I didn't bother to ask my cousin for the money because I still had the money I was managing, and I knew my cousin was routinely sending the money back home to my parents.

Three weeks before I had to do my visa change, my cousin told me to see him so we could manage to pay for my flight, and he also told me to bring the salary that I had received. I was dumbfounded because I knew my agent was sending my money directly to him since I could not open an account with a tourist visa. I told him exactly what my agent told me, and he said the same thing. So, since he could speak the Thai language well, he called the agent, and she said she had already transferred my salary to me. I went straight to my director and narrated what was going on. He called the agent, and the agent said she gave all my salary to my cousin, and my director believed her at that time.

The agent's betrayal agitated me; already, I was low on funds, and the salary was supposed to meet my flight expenses, yet I had not received it. As my cousin and I were in a rush, we decided to take immediate action and engage in conversation with the school's top management.

My cousin called my head of department and spoke with him; then he showed all the messages in which the agent told him that she had given me my salary, and I showed my director and my head of department the messages she sent to me. At that moment, they believed us, and they told the woman that they would fire her. Meanwhile, when they told her that, she threatened me with immigration because, under normal circumstances, I was not supposed to be working with a tourist visa. Moreover, there were certain documents that she had to return so that I could do my visa change; she refused to return the documents, and I had only three days left to go do the visa change.

My director saw my frustration and decided to hire me directly that same day. They prepared all the necessary documents and gave me money to assist me with my flight expenses. All of this was no less than a miracle; just a few days before the visa change, I was puzzled, uncertain, and annoyed when, all of a sudden, assistance from the director came at the right time. To this day, I am still thankful for what they did for me in the moment of adversity. With their help, I finally traveled to Malaysia, changed my visa, and came back to Thailand.

Nine months passed, and I was unable to pay even up to $700 of my debt back home. I knew the only way for me to pay the debt was to seek an opportunity and move elsewhere. Fortunately, an opportunity came up to travel to South Korea, and I grabbed it.

At first in South Korea, things didn't just become better for me. I suffered a lot in the beginning. This was because I had no one there nor any friends. So, I went on Facebook and searched for Cameroonians living in South Korea, and among the people I saw, the spirit of God led me to a certain lady of my age. I spoke to her and explained my situation to her; I also told her I needed help because I was moving there with no place to stay. She directed me to a company that provides accommodations. I traveled to Korea, followed her directions, and finally approached the company. They took me to an apartment with two rooms and sixteen people in there, and I was the 17th.

It was a hassle because I had nothing to sleep on, and the place was very congested. I remembered the struggle: I had to put on a jacket and sleep on the floor for two weeks straight before the company could find another place for six of us. You might be thinking that it would have weakened me, but no, the struggle actually made me stronger. I worked harder, finished paying off my debt back home, and now I could look for a place of my own.

I was an asylum seeker in South Korea, and it is exceedingly difficult for them to grant asylum. I anticipated the scenario and decided that I would have to relocate to another country sooner. So, I just lived there for four years because that was the amount of time I had on my ID card. In those four years, I had collected ample funds to bear to manage immediate expenses and also had extra cash too.

When my time was up in South Korea, immigration issued me an exit letter with a month of validity. In Korea, as per the regulations, a person cannot leave the airport with more than $10,000, and if an individual wants to carry more than that amount, they must declare it. I had more than $10,000, and I decided to buy goods and cars, which I shipped before leaving for Cameroon.

While in Cameroon, I enjoyed every moment there with families and friends. I was meeting my loved ones after a long time, and surely, it was an emotional time for me. When my goods arrived, I sold them and recovered my money. Everything was going pretty well for me; I was joyous and had money until a political strike broke up in the English part of Cameroon, where the population was against the government.

Due to the political unrest, many people died; this was on the 1st of October 2017 I am talking about; the fight is still going on till now (11th of April 2024). Hundreds of thousands of people have died as of today and almost a million of them have been internally displaced.

Sometime in October of 2017, I met a girl named Bertsey Bright, and we fell in love. We had good and intimate times, which led to her getting pregnant. She was a third-year student at SOA University in Yaoundé the capital city of Cameroon. When she broke the news to me, I was excited, but she was nervous and scared because of her family and since it was important for her family that she didn't get pregnant out of wedlock. Her friends in school advised her to terminate the pregnancy; they also told her that I was going to abandon her and run away.

My love told me about what all of her friends said about me. It didn't make me angry, although I felt the urge to travel from the Northwest region of the country to the central part of the country to meet with her and her friends and to prove that all their assumptions they had about me were wrong.

When I arrived at SOA, I rested there for a couple of days. Then, I took my girl and all her friends out to spend money on food and drinks for them. They were excited and satisfied, and we left for their school hostel. My girl and I went to bed; the next morning, while I was still sleeping, she had already woken up and was outside discussing with her friends about the previous night. By then, all of Bertsey's friends had stated that they liked me; they also told her that I was responsible and that she should keep the pregnancy. I had now won the trust of all of her friends.

Everything was really going fine for us, but we had a big problem, which was to break the pregnancy news to her parents. Bertsey's family had a strict stance on pregnancy outside of wedlock; along with her, I was hesitant too to tell them about our situation and was looking for the right moment, and we decided to delay the matter until then.

Since the political struggle was still going on, I went back to where I was residing. Because of the struggle, I got arrested by the military. I was locked up in prison and was brutally tortured there, even though I was completely innocent. The prison was a tight and small facility that could hold up to about 150 people max, but we were about a thousand of us in there. It was jammed-packed, and one couldn't imagine how I survived there.

The prison also did not have any sleeping spaces or any toilets. We used buckets as toilets; before dawn, we had to take the mess out. My uncle and a human rights advocate helped me to escape from prison. They paid an English-speaking warden for my release, and he helped me to flee from prison. On the night of my release, the said warden ordered me to take the buckets of poop and throw it. When we were at the place where we dumped the poop, he told me to run away. At first, I was scared that he wanted to kill me because that had happened before, but he informed me that my uncle and the human rights advocate had arranged for my release.

When I escaped that night, the next day, I found myself in a small village where I was there for a week. I borrowed a phone, called my family, and explained my situation. My family looked for money and sent it to me, which I used to travel to Nigeria.

My time in Nigeria wasn't very calm either. After a few days in Nigeria, Boko Haram, a terrorist group, attacked where we lived. By now, you would have known that matters had become life-threatening, to the point that I was forced to return to Cameroon and remained underground till my uncle was able to help me leave the country.

Before leaving the country, I spoke with my girl and decided to tell her family about her condition. I thought it was the right time to engage with her family, but I was entirely wrong. Bertsey's family didn't take the news of their daughter's pregnancy well; after learning about it, they were outraged and drove me and my mother out of their house. I went to my girl's place and spent four days with her until it was time for me to travel out of the country; I traveled to Ecuador.

Ecuador is a Visa-free country, along with Cameroon, which made it easier for me to go there. While in Ecuador, I met a lady named Cissé Sarah. Cissé owned multiple businesses there. I was lodging in one of her hotels and would buy food from her restaurant. In her hotel, I met three other guys from Cameroon (two were from the French part of Cameroon, and the other was from the English part of Cameroon).

I befriended the English-speaking guy; we did everything together until one day, I do not know how he got to know I had money, and he started telling stories about how Cissé Sarah had connections to help people go to Mexico through the ship for the cost of $1,500.

Once I learned that Cissé could help me leave Ecuador, I became invested in this opportunity. As I couldn't speak and understand Spanish, I told my friend to beg the lady that I was interested. The very next day after the discussion with my friend, Cissé Sarah met us and brought up the same topic but told me that the chance was only for one person, and she wanted to involve only my friend; I again insisted that she should look for a way to include me, since I had the money on me, and she told me that she was going to work a way out.

Two days passed by, and Sarah asked me for $1,500 to secure my spot; I immediately gave her the money, and she told the two of us to prepare because she was going to take us to the person who was going to help us board on the ship to Mexico. The D-day finally arrived, and she came for us. She took us by taxi to another city, and we met one short, fat, and rounded man named Francis, who was in his late thirties. Francis took us to his house to meet another guy. We were at his place for almost two hours, and he took us to a bus station where he told us to pay our bus fare. We paid for our bus fare, and he paid for his, and we traveled to another city. We arrived at that city around 1:30 AM; he took us to a nearby Bush and asked us to hide there because the police of that city hated immigrants; upon seeing us, they could either arrest or torture us, which could eventually result in blowing our immigration efforts.

Francis took $100 each from the three of us, saying he would pay for our bus fare to Columbia, and that was the place where we were to take the ship. Francis paid for the bus fare, but the bus fare was not even up to $25 per person. I know a lot of you would be asking how we knew the bus fare was not up to $25 since we were hiding in the bus. Well, I am going to answer your question; the driver that was going to carry us had seen what was going on long ago before Francis walked up to the place where tickets were being sold. While we were in the Bush, one police officer saw us and walked to us, asking what we were doing there in Spanish, but we could not understand. The driver who was going to take us came to our rescue and spoke with the police officer, and the police officer left.

We followed the driver to get onto the bus, but we did not even know where Francis was. So, the driver told us that Francis was an unbelievably lousy guy since he saw Francis take $100 each from us. We never confronted Francis because we knew he was trying to help us travel to Mexico, and the remaining balance would be his compensation for supporting us. Finally, we traveled and arrived in Columbia, and we took a cab to Buenaventura around the coast of Columbia.

We took a hotel in Buenaventura, and we were there for three weeks since Francis said the ship that would carry us had not arrived. Every other day, we would walk to the coast side to check on the ship and see if the ship was around. It was a tense period and a test of our patience; the three-week time might not seem to be a big deal for most of you, but remember that we were in a foreign land with limited cash, unaware of the native language, and at any time if we would have been caught the things might have taken a turn for the worst.

One faithful day, we left for the coast to check for the ship, and we found one ship miles away sailing in our direction as we thought. We returned to the hotel to pack our stuff and were all set to be on board. Francis asked us for $1,500 each for ship fare, and we were confused since we had already paid Sarah. An argument broke out between us and Francis. Francis told us that Sarah only gave him just $600, and he had spent a lot of money on the way with us.

Meanwhile, it was all lies since we paid for our car fares and food. He made us believe that if we did not board that ship, we would have to wait for a month for the ship to go back. I have never been so furious with my life as that day. We tried calling Sarah to verify what Francis said about her not receiving money from her, but her number was not going through; if it did go through, she would not answer. I did not have the money he asked for again, and I had to start thinking about how to come about with the amount. At that moment, I knew Sarah had conned me, but an idea came to my mind: I should call my mum to start looking for money to borrow and send to me to continue my journey.

My mum means the world to me because that same day, she tried to borrow about $1,100; my junior brother helped me with $200, and my friend Eric, who was in South Korea, helped me with $200. With God's blessing and the help of my family and friends, I managed to have enough cash to give to Francis so that I could get on board. That moment taught me a great lesson about life: "Always be kind to people because you do not know where or when you will meet or need their help."

I gave Francis another $1,500 to pay for the ship, and he left us at the hotel. Francis told us that he would arrange for our transportation. Francis returned in the evening and took us towards the loading dock for a ferry. There, he showed us a ship that was far in the water and told us that we would take that same ship to Mexico City. We believed him since we saw the ship; from there, we went back to the hotel, where we started packing our bags.

The night passed, morning came, and it was time for us to go. Francis took us to that ferry loading dock, and we took a ferry that was available there, thinking it was going to the ship. Francis knew everything that was happening. The ferry was going to a nearby island, and that was its last destination. The ferry dropped us off on that island and headed back to where it took us. Francis told us to follow him; he looked for a motel to spend the night there and continue the journey the next day.

The plan was for us to sleep at that motel, wake up exceedingly early, and take a boat to the ship that we saw. Francis left for the hotel we were in before traveling to the island. Little did we know that the ship we saw was moving, so morning came, and we woke up to find no ship in the water. We called Francis, and he told us to be ready because a boat was coming for us, which did come for us, and we entered the boat. Guess what? The boat was just a fishing boat with two people inside it, and those two guys spoke only Spanish. We were baffled at that time because we knew the boat could not carry many people. Besides, I didn't know who could speak or even understand Spanish. If you are wondering why we got on the boat, then know that it was our only option to get out of the Island and somehow continue the journey.

Fortunately, one of my friends knew Spanish, and those guys told us that we would be in that boat for eight hours a day, and then we were going to arrive in Mexico City, which was a big lie. We started the journey around 7 AM, and if you do the math, eight hours was supposed to be by 3 PM, but it was more than 3 PM, and I told my friends that we were going to sleep in that boat because I could not see land. All my eyes could see, no matter how far I looked, was just water. Before I continue, go to your Google map and search for Buenaventura in Columbia. You will see it is near the Pacific Ocean, which means the water we were traveling inside with no life jackets was the Pacific Ocean, and we did not know.

Back to the struggle, around 6 PM, after I had told my friends we were going to sleep in that boat, those two guys took out a mini stove and fried us plantains and fish that they caught, and we ate. After eating, they arranged a place for us to sleep since it was getting dark. Sleeping in the dark at that time reminded me some way or another about my time in jail. There were many similarities that I could have drawn out; there was the fear of the unknown, lack of control, confinement, and vulnerability. Although the biggest fear of them all was what if a thunderstorm would occur and end our lives in a snap second? It was fair to assume that as we were in the Pacific.

At 10 PM, the boat was switched off. and we slept. It was so peaceful and scary at the same time, but we had no choice. Around 5 AM, they started the boat for us to continue the journey, and around 10 AM, another boat came for us. The give and take from one boat to another lasted for three days, and the last board came for us on the fourth day. Do you know that we were in the Pacific Ocean without lifesaving jackets? None of us were proficient swimmers and prolonged exposure to cold water could have caused hypothermia. If any of the boats on which we were traveling had sunk, then we would have been swept away by the strong currents of the Oceans. See how much we risked our lives just in the name of going to Mexico City.

On the fourth day, the last boat came for us, and it was a flying boat. We hopped in and had the scariest moments of our lives because this boat was going up and down like a ball thrown from the sky. I see why they named those equipment flying boats; they really can fly. It was among the most horrifying moments of my life; I was holding onto the ledges of the boat as if my life depended on it. While we were in that boat, it also started to rain heavily; the whole scene was no less than a thunderstorm, just which I feared the most. The guys who were sailing stopped the boat, made phone calls, and looked around the water; they were also terrified by the scene. However, my friends and I were naïve in witnessing the terrors of the ocean, and the only thing left for us was to start praying since we knew that it could be our end. When praying, I also thought about my family and how their prayers could have been answered by God and come to my rescue.

The guys sailing our boat chose one direction; perhaps it was their intuition or experience. After choosing the direction, they followed its path until we escaped the rain. There, we saw a shocking natural phenomenon that we were neither able to comprehend nor explain, i.e., we saw two different water bodies, one of which was dark blue and the other dirty brown, and they did not mix. When I first saw it, it felt like an illusion to me; it was as if an invisible barricade held two water bodies apart.

As we continued our journey, we saw something like land and were so happy that we were almost arriving at our destination. I was overjoyed, and so was my friend, and we had all the reasons to be happy after trembling in the ocean for hours and risking our lives. It took us about six hours to arrive at what we thought was land, and to our surprise, all we could see was an excessively big piece of stone. All of our hopes were shattered.

If you could rate the disappointment on our faces on a scale of 1 to 100, you would give us 100. We continued our journey and saw a boat far away. We were scared that it was the Marines or Coast guards, but God was there for us; it was some tourist on tour; we all were calmed and sailed away.

As we rode past tourist for about 500 meters, we saw the threat. This time, it really was the Marines and the Coast guards mixed together; we all were frightened as we saw them; our fear spiked at that time because if they had caught us, our whole immigration journey would have ended in jeopardy, but miraculously, the Marines and the Coast guards didn't see us, and we continued our journey. The two guys controlling the flying boats took one route, which led us to the bank of the sea. Actually, getting to the bank was a big problem since the wave was too strong, but eventually, we succeeded.

Those guys told us to keep walking by the bank, and someone was coming for us; we walked for almost 20 minutes, and we saw one old man in his late fifties or early sixties, and he took us to his house. The man was a total stranger to us; we had no idea what he could do to my friend and me, as we were both helpless at that time, and we were dependent on him. I wished everything to turn out to be fine, as we had already taken a rollercoaster ride throughout our journey in the ocean, encompassing different experiences, most of which were bone-chilling.

The man who hosted us was married, but he didn't have any children. To my surprise, he and his wife didn't make any compromise in our hospitality, and in the trustiest sense, they treated us like their own children. All of my doubts that I previously had of being hosted by a stranger vanished because of his respect for us and assistance in our time of need. Although we had language barriers, we lived with them with peace, harmony, and happiness. We were with them for six days, and the old couple made us feel at home.

We tried calling Francis to confront him with the risk he put into our lives. Francis told us that if he had told us about the journey, we would not have taken the risk. Francis's response infuriated us, and moreover, we were also constantly livid with the ambiguity of the whole situation. We yelled at Francis and asked for the next step forward and he told us that someone was coming for us the next day, which was the seventh day.

After we called Francis, he said that the two guys from the flying boats would come and ask us for $150 so the police would not come to disturb us. That was our translation of what we understood they were saying, and we gave them the money. We weren't sure at that time whether it was to pay off the police or any reason, but at that time, we had to do what they told us. Otherwise, the situation could have turned out to be even worse. I had no money on me, but I told my friends to take care of everything, and when we arrived where we could receive money, I would contact my family to send me money to repay them. He agreed to it, and we were all prepared to continue our journey.

The seventh day arrived, and that old man came and woke us up by 5 AM. We took our things and headed somewhere we did not know. We walked for two hours, and this old man kept us beside a riverbank. We sat there for one more hour, and a canoe with an engine came for us. We hopped in that canoe, and man started heading west. Suddenly, he stopped the canoe and asked us for $450, or else we would get off his canoe. The demand for such an amount left me and my friend in utter shock. We had anticipated $150 for the police, and what the man demanded was way more than that.

We begged and begged, but he was headstrong and told us to get down or pay him if we wanted to continue the journey on the boat. The situation got tense as time passed; we were in the water body and could not swim. Fortunately, my friends paid for the trip, and we continued the journey. I couldn't have thanked him more as he was the person who bailed us out in such a tense and adverse situation. We were very relieved, but we both were also mindful of the fact that we were losing big bucks as the journey continued.

When the water was shallow, we decided that we would jump into the river and give the canoe a push. We did this for hours upon hours until we arrived at a small village where this guy took us there and introduced us to the villagers and gave money to two boys aged 17 and 19 and he told us to wait in one the houses for those boys to take us and continue the journey. It was another unknown place and circumstance we were in, and again, I made a call to prayers from God. Until those two boys returned, we rested inside the house, completely exhausted from the journey.

It was 2 PM, and those two boys came and told us it was time for them to take us to Panama City and that it was an hour's walk. The constant back and forth throughout the journey was a grind; thankfully, the rest we had taken earlier helped us to energize. We headed out for the journey, and all these guys took was an empty container, a small pack of rice, a small pot, a small machete, and a lighter.

The two young boys told us to walk faster so that we could be out of the jungle before nightfall. We walked as fast as we could and made it out of the jungle by nightfall to a small house that we found. In that house, we saw a big family consisting of grandma, grandpa, parents, and children. They welcomed us well, and their hospitality proved to be wholesome.

Our hosts were uncivilized, or it would be better if I say primitive, because the women had no dress on top, and their breasts were all outside. Their clothing was shabby, and they also had no light and had never seen a mobile phone. After seeing them, I was bewildered and wondered that people like these still exist. But what surprised me even more was that with such fewer resources and dire poverty, they were still willing to help us and make us feel at home.

We spent the night with them in their small house. We had good times, too; even though we could not understand each other, we communicated with signs. My time with them taught me how big their hearts were and how much they cared for us. Their wealth might seem minimal, but in the true sense, they were still benevolent.

Morning came, and it was time to head out and continue the journey. To be honest, if people in South America tell you good morning, check your watch because these boys said it was a six-hour journey, but it later became a four-day walk. We started the journey and walked continually for some time without keeping track of it; we had only aimed to walk no matter how exhausting the journey got. After a long and tiring walk, we came across a river with an extraordinarily strong current.

After we saw the river, my friend and I were in awe of nature. Not only was it flowing at a threatening speed, but its water was at my neck level, too. The strong and fast current and considerable depth was evident, and there was no way that my friend and I could swim through it. Fortunately, the two boys who were accompanying us on the journey were native and hence great swimmers. First looked for a long stick and helped us cross.

We continued until we saw a big mountain to climb, and we decided to take a rest. Those guys brought out the pot and the pack of rice, which we boiled and shared without any source or soup. As hungry as we were, that rice was the best thing we could ever wish for; it was at that moment through which I embraced the magic simplicity. The tranquility of eating the meal and resting after the enervating journey helped us to catch some breath and invigorate.

After eating, we headed up the mountain, and it took us four hours to climb up and four hours to go down. While up there, we encountered wildlife that we did not mess with, and we were just praying that they would not have an encounter with us, and they did not. The journey we were on was just a test of our stamina and patience, but it was also a trail of our bravery. As we crossed through the lush and green mountain, we made sure not to panic as doing so would have caught the attention of any dangerous animal.

God was always there with us at every part of the journey, and it proved so as we safely passed the mountain. When night came, we looked for plantain leaves and made a little bed to sleep in. We made a fire to keep us warm, and the two boys went to a river close by. They caught fish, which we roasted and ate. The meal was simple yet delightful and nutritious. On the journey, we all enjoyed the timely pauses of meals; it improved our mood, provided us a sense of comfort in challenging times, and gave us much- needed mental alertness to continue our journey.

Morning came, and we continued our journey; another day passed, and we slept in the jungle. On the fourth day of our journey, we arrived at a little river, and those two boys told us that they could not continue until we paid them again. They asked for $70, and we had just a $100 bill, and they did not have change, so we decided to give them things that could make up the money they asked for. As they agreed to settle for something other than the money, it relieved us; this was because we were short on cash already, and as we had a long way to go, we knew that we would need some spare money to pay off any unforeseen expense.

We gave the boys expensive clothes and a bag pack, which they collected, and we continued the journey for about three hours. The further the journey continued, the more it took a mental and physical toll on us, but we were also determined to strive and survive through our course.

After three hours, the boys told us it was the end of the line for them. They could not go further because we were closer to Panama's borders, and it would be illegal for them, and they might go to jail. We understood their constraints and didn't want to put their lives at risk at our expense. Finally, after a long stretch, the boys parted ways with us; we did thank them, as without them, we wouldn't have accomplished a considerable part of our journey.

Before departing, the boys who accompanied us on the journey directed us about the route to Panama. We continued without them for about three more hours. Then came a river, but it was not very steep. We easily crossed the river and entered Panama. Trust me, making it to Panama was excruciatingly difficult; just give it a thought that we crossed a perilous river, hiked for eight hours through a mountainous jungle, crossed a river again, and walked miles and hours of which I couldn't keep a count of.

We walked for about thirty minutes and came to an army barracks. If you are wondering how we got caught so easily, then know that several barracks and troops patrol the borders. We would have been caught one way or the other. Anyway, the troops took us in; they were also kind enough to give us bread and water. We savagely ate the bread and swiftly gulped the water because we were famished and parched.

The troops processed us and told us that the President of Panama asked us to return and take the normal route that immigrants always take. To put it simply, what the troops meant was to reroute the journey all the way; after listening to this, we were astonished; there was no way we were going to head back and risk our lives in risk again, and by now, we had minimal cash to spend. We had no other option than to resist their orders; this eventually led the troops to pull their guns on us. We were scared, and our last resort was to save our lives and head back.

Before we left, we asked them for a box of matches so that anywhere night falls, we could make fire and sleep. Heading out, we crossed the same river before meeting with those troops. We got wet trying to cross the river, and the matches were all soaked, so we decided to wait by the riverbank and dry up the matches. It was very disappointing for me and my friend, as we risked and struggled too much to get to Panama, and we had to head back. But as the old saying goes, "When there is a will, there's a way." And God paved the way for us.

While waiting for the matches to dry up, we heard a bark-like sound, and all of a sudden, we were taken back at first and frightened; we thought it might be a menacing creature, but to our surprise, it was a dog and with whom there was a hunter. We offered the hunter $100 to show us the way to Panama City, which he did show the way to go to Panama City.

As we were moving in the direction the hunter navigated us through the journey, I heard a boat, and my instinct told me it was those military guys looking for us. Believing my guts, I told my friends that we should hide, and they said we should call for help instead. I insisted, and they finally listened. As soon as we hid, there was the military in the boat passing by, my friends were suspicious for a moment. If anyone feels something is not right, then we should all agree with that person. And so, we all hid, which saved our lives.

We continued walking until we saw an angle. We asked for his help, and he agreed to show us how we could use Panama City. He told us to pay him, and we agreed. He took us to a village and said that the people in that village would help us. It was time for his payment. We only had $100 bills on us, and he refused the money and asked for jewelry. I gave him my $100 watch and some clothes. The watch was both expensive and important to me, but as you know, nothing at that time felt more vital than reaching Panama City.

As we entered the village, we met a man in his early thirties and tried to explain where we were heading. He said the military warned them never to help immigrants. He offered us some fried plantains and eggs, and he also showed us where we could take a shower. I had the utmost respect for that man; part of the reason was that he was still helping us out in our time of need; moreover, he was also risking his life because if the military had caught him, he could have been in danger along with us.

The man later took us to the grandma, who spoke only Spanish. She brought out a Spanish Bible, and we read Psalms 91 to her and other villagers who came around. It was one of the most harmonious and spiritual moments of my journey, and you would also be right to think that such a moment uplifted and motivated me.

After reading that verse in the Bible, Grandma spoke with the guy we met. She asked about us from the person who accompanied us. They were talking in Spanish. We didn't know exactly what they were talking about, but from the facial expression I read, Grandma had a kind of motherly emotion and a sense of goodwill depicting us. We took Grandma's blessing and headed on.

The man who accompanied us told us that he would help us up to another village where we would take a ship to Panama City, but it would cost us $60 to fuel a boat. We gave him $100, and he left and returned hours later, saying that there was no change and that we couldn't travel until he got the change. This left us again in a whirlpool of confusion and complication; my friends and I knew that it was not good that we kept losing cash like that, no matter whether it was even a few bucks.

We had to swallow the hard pill, and for the sake of continuing the journey, we told the man to keep the change and take us to where he was taking us. We traveled for three hours in the boat and arrived at the village by 10 PM, and as God does his things, the coast guards were not even available at the place where the boat stopped. It sure did was something that not me but my friends could sense, that we had an invisible aid that paved our journey easier by eradicating the barriers, and it sure did was God because the water bodies near the border are highly patrolled, and due to some coincidence or miracle the troops were not there when we were traveling.

We entered the village, met a couple, and asked them to show us a hotel or motel. They took us to one motel owned by a white Hispanic lady, and she said she does not accept Black people at her motel. This was a shocking experience for me; I don't know what might be the reason for this act, but it was discriminatory. No one of my friends, me, nor the couple who accompanied us resisted her because we knew that it wouldn't have changed her ignorance and bigotry.

One of the couples (the man) told us that he would instead take us to a Black-owned motel. He took us there, and this lady welcomed us. We explained what we wanted to the lady, and she told us that the ship in that village leaves once a week and only comes back one week after. She said we were late to board the ship, meaning we must be in that village for one week. We all agreed that one week would give us ample time to take a much-needed break and prepare for the later part of the journey.

There was a military barrack closer to the motel, and the lady told us that to be safe, we should spend the whole week inside the motel, and whatever we needed, she was going to assign someone to help us. Although we could have exhibited some mobility, we didn't want any trouble for us and her. She helped provide everything we wanted until the last day when the ship came.

We gave the lady money to buy us breakfast, and she never showed up until after 3 PM. We told her to return the money, and she did. Later, two of my friends decided to buy food and tickets, and we were going to board the ship to Panama City. We all had everything planned out; just after a matter of time, we would have been boarded on the ship all the way to Panama City, but little did we know that a rug was about to be pulled out from under us.

That was the very first day my friends headed out from the hotel. The military guys arrested them. I waited for them until my instinct told me to go peep at the balcony, which I did, and I saw them coming from a distance with two military guys. I took that brief time to pack everything because I knew they were coming for me. They came for me and took us three to the hospital and, after, straight to jail. At that moment, I felt that it might be all over because the military had caught us a second time; they might be more rigid and strict with their actions.

We were jailed for one week, and one day, a helicopter came to that village. It was a Lieutenant Colonel and some charity organization. The Lieutenant told us that the President of Panama asked us to go back. Again, our journey was near jeopardy. The Lieutenant told us that they would send us back the next day. It might be all over, but my friends and I weren't giving up so easily, and after much thoughts, we strategized a plan that would help us delay the deportation process by attempting to commit suicide. I know this act is not preferable in any situation, but we also had no other alternatives.

So, we went to shower, took the soap, and put in an empty water bottle. We came to our cell unit and mixed the soap with some medications from the hospital, and we gave the oldest person amongst us to ingest. After he ingested the mixture, my other friend and I began to scream that our friend was dying, and they took him to the hospital. This plan made those military guys angry; they were infuriated and took everything that we could use to harm ourselves and started treating us very poorly, but for us, the plan worked because the deportation was further delayed.

After my friend left the hospital, the doctor followed him to our cell, and we explained to those military guys that we were merely immigrants, and we were just passing through that village to Panama City. The doctor talked with those military guys, and they kept going back and forth until he left. There was a God-fearing military guy who loved us when he came to give us food; in the challenging situation we were in, he was one true saint for us who helped us as a fellow human and earned the respect of my respect. Not only did he help us with food, but he also informed us about the next possible course of action. He told us that he had overheard the Lieutenant say they would let us go, but he did not know if we were going to Panama City or back to Columbia.

At 5 AM the following morning, we heard a knock on our door cell. It was one of the military guys who told us to go shower, which we did, and they gave us food. From the moment I woke up until the time of the meal, I was perplexed about whether we were going to our destination or back to Colombia. The former was preferable, and the latter was highly undesirable for us.

The moment for the release finally came, they took us by the riverbank, and we met an English-speaking girl. The girl asked us why we were locked up, and we explained. She whispered to us that she heard that we were going with them to Panama City via a military boat. We were overjoyed, but we did not want to show it.

We finally made it to Panama City, and they took us to an immigration camp there; we were there for three days. We were then transported with about sixty other immigrants to the Panama and Costa Rica border. An immigration officer came to the border and took us to Costa Rica. My friends and I were satisfied by now because we were closer to our final destination as the journey progressed; we were moving further up north from Latin America to the US.

We were at the immigration camp in Costa Rica, waiting for them to process us so that we could continue our journey to other countries. The next day, they released us, and we moved north of Costa Rica, where we met a lady popularly known as Mama Africa. She accommodated us for one night and asked each of us to pay $450 to be transported from Nicaragua to Honduras.

When Mama Africa requested $450, I was ambushed, not because the money was too much but because neither my friend nor I had any money. I thought about what to do, and finally, I came up with the only viable solution: asking my mother for the money. My mother then sent me money through Western Union. I collected the money and paid for the two of us because one of my friends spent his money all the time we were traveling with me.

It was 10 PM, and Mama Africa came to us and told us it was time to go. We took a bus to a sea bank and waited till midnight when some men working for her came to us and gave us yellow wristbands to identify us. At the sea bank, three boats came, and we were to board seventeen in each per boat, but we did not board all the boats because there were other groups of people there from another agent.

The men working for Mama Africa stopped the boats from leaving and started looking at our wrists to identify us. They made everyone with the yellow wristband enter the boat. Another boat came for the other immigrants, and we headed straight into the sea. We sailed until 4 AM when our fuel ran out. The sudden stoppage of the journey just terrified us all; we were in the middle of the sea, totally unaware of countless threats, until the testament of our patience and stress escalated further, and the rescue came in time.

As there were other boats, too, our sailor communicated the situation to them, and they came to our aid and gave us fuel to continue. We continued for about 15 minutes, and we arrived in Nicaragua. We were in a different country now, which meant we had to constantly be altered from the border patrolling troops and marines.

But at the given time, it was not the troops that were the threat but the robber. The sailors told us to run into the bushes because they saw armed robbers who fired a gun at us. My heart was pounding in that state. I was not alone, and the other along with me were petrified and scared to death. One bullet could have ended the life of one of us.

If you are wondering why the robbers were after us, it was because these armed robbers knew Mama Africa gave one of the immigrants a huge sum of money to give to the other agents in Nicaragua, but they did not know the exact person. So, they chased us that night, and we succeeded in escaping and hiding. We remained hiding until 6 AM, when a cargo truck came for us and took us to a deserted bush, where we stayed until 7 PM. All of us felt so lucky that we had chased a major threat, and we were relaxed once we got on the truck.

The truck came for us early that same evening around 7 PM with two other trucks, and they transported us. On our way, we had a flat tire, and the driver stopped and told us to be quiet because a police officer was coming by with a K-9 dog. We all feared and even held our breath; we made sure that there was dead silence, but the patrol dog smelled our scent and started to bark loudly.

To this day, I still don't know if one of Mama Africa's guys gave the police officer money or not because the dog could scent us, and the police officer didn't bother to interrogate the vehicle. After some time, he left, and we continued our journey to a remote location, where we started walking with one of Mama Africa's men. We didn't know where we were heading, and we were also tired; just in the few previous days, we had crossed a country, chased patrolling cops and marines, and robbers, too.

The man working for Mama Africa was with us and took us for an hour-long walk or more. After that, we met another Mama Africa's man who took over and continued with us. The journey continued until we arrived in Honduras by 5 AM. The journey became easier as we entered Honduras. We took a bus to the immigration and waited for one day until they gave us a pass to continue.

As the pass came, we took a bus to the Guatemala border. The immigration gave us another pass, which we used to reach the border between Guatemala and Mexico. We arrived at the border by midnight and looked for an inn to spend the night. We rested there, having no clear plan in mind for ahead, but we focused on getting some rest first and later deciding on what to do.

When we were in the hotel, a native guy walked up to us and told us to give him $5 each so that he could take us to Mexico. But we were so scared that we told him to come the next day; what scared us was that the person was a total stranger to us, and neither did we know what his intentions were. But the point of thinking further was long gone when he came to us the following day. He then accompanied us and we began the journey.

The man took us to a point where we had to cross a river. There, he asked for the money we gave him, and he arranged with some guys to cross us over. The river was quite difficult for us to pass; it was fast-flowing and had a considerable depth; only the natives could have known how to pass by it, and that is where the man who accompanied us made himself useful.

After we crossed the river, we took tricycles to the bus stop, and from there, we took the bus to the immigration camp in Tapachula, but they were all closed for the day to process us, and they told us to look for a hotel and come back the next day.

The next day, we went there, and they took us in. I stayed there for seven days, where I was interviewed and released with one of my friends. After we were released, we stayed in an unbelievably cheap hotel for about three days while waiting for my friend's brother to pay us a flight to Mexicali. The brother decided to pay mine because I helped his brother throughout the journey by motivating him, helping him with his bag, and more.

His brother paid for a first-class flight for us, and as soon as we arrived in Mexicali, my friend and I enjoyed a fine time in the fight after days of rigorous effort. To me, it truly felt like a supreme luxury, and we made no mistake in enjoying such comfort. We were in a state of utmost tranquility on the flight. Little did we know that something unexpected was about to occur, and something unfortunate happened.

As we landed at the airport, we got arrested again, and we were taken by the police as if we were criminals. After all the treatments, we were transported to the border between Mexico and America, and we got locked up there for a day and were released the next day.

We looked around and saw an exceedingly lengthy line of three entering a gate, and when we asked, we were told they were entering to work in California. We joined the lines, and when it was our turn to identify ourselves at the gate, we showed our Cameroon ID's. Not up to one minute, the whole area was covered with police officers, and we got arrested again, and we were transported upstairs, where we spent three days there. The way we were being treated was bizarre. Often, it felt like discrimination; the sad part was that the police officer wasn't also showing any remorse for their actions.

We got interviewed and processed, and after that, we were transported to the Imperial Correctional Facility, where I was there for three months and 21 days (about fifteen weeks). While in the facility, I met an immigration lawyer called Elizabeth Lopez. Elizabeth was a kind lady; she had treated me and my friend in a very calm manner. It felt like she was God-sent in my life to help me rescue, so I put my trust in her and decided only she would represent me in the immigration case.

She went through my story and told me that I had a very strong case and that I stood a 90% chance of winning my asylum case. She asked me for Two Thousand Dollars ($2,000) for her to represent me. That was quite a hefty amount for us to manage; by the time of our trial, I hadn't had a dime on me, but I was also not to give up on the immigration, given that I was so close to my goal.

We settled on a contract: I would provide her with Five Hundred Dollars upfront and pay the rest in installments. She was kind enough to understand my situation and agree on payment through installments. I couldn't have been much happier, but somehow, I had to pay the $500 upfront payment first.

To pay the $500 upfront charge, I called my parents back home; although they never had money then, my mum called one of her friends in Maryland and explained my situation to her. She told my mum to give me her number so that I could call her. Aunt Prudence is her name, and she has a heart of gold. I called her, we spoke, and to my greatest surprise, she sent me six hundred fifty dollars ($650) to pay the lawyer and get myself some toiletries. It felt like I had received something better than aid. Also, the extra $150 she sent me just showed how much she cherished and cared for me.

I respect these two ladies whom God placed in my life to help me in many ways. I went through all the court proceedings, and in the end, I was granted asylum and released. That day, I was delighted and excited, and it felt like a victory. That day, I realized that all my efforts in the tough immigration journeys were paid off. I was now where I wanted to be.

After I was released and months passed by, the lawyer called me and told me, "Know that you have found a sister in the United States, and if there is any issue that you face, do not hesitate to get to me, and I have a gift for you, the One Thousand and Five Hundred Dollars, you owe me, use it and apply for your Green Card." Trust me, her words did wonder to me; there was no better gift I could have asked or wished for. My respect for her transcended to a whole new level; she did not just say to be my sister but also acted like one. It felt like a miracle that she was ready to help me so much. Who says God does not work in a mysterious way?

Sometimes in life, we are quick to judge people; why do I say this? My cousin agreed to help when I got to the States by sheltering me, and when I needed him, he was disconnected. I concluded that he was just being wicked to me, not knowing what he was going through then.

My girlfriend's sister gave me all the help I could ever wish for; to date, this lady is my elder sister, my mentor, my destiny helper, my mother in the States, and in fact, my everything. She has a heart of pure gold, is exceedingly kind and humble, and is always ready to help even if she has nothing. This lady is a rare germ; many people cannot understand what I mean until you cross paths with sister Blessing.

She housed me, fed me, assisted me by paying part of my school fees, and took care of my family back in Cameroon when I could not. People say that she did all this because I had a child with her younger sister, but, NO, she is just like that in real nature. Moreover, this lady helped me look for jobs until I finally got one, and she told me not to pay rent or any bills but to concentrate on taking care of my family. This is just a tip of how nice this lady was and is still lovely, with a beautiful soul.

I worked hard for four years and saved money to do things right with my girlfriend by putting a ring on her finger. But, since I was an asylum seeker, I cannot return home till I become a citizen of the

United States. The only way I could see them was to move them to another country and meet them there, which I did.

I planned to meet my girlfriend in Rwanda since it is a visa-free country for Cameroon. Before my girlfriend and daughter could come to Rwanda, I had to send her to Congo to do some documents there. All the trips, including my trip to Rwanda and back, not forgetting housing and feeding expenses, cost about $13,000. I did not mind spending that amount of money, and do you know why? Here you go; I spent that amount of money because I had not seen my girlfriend for four years, and I had never seen my daughter since I left when her mother was three months pregnant.

My girlfriend and daughter missed their flight, which was a non-refundable flight, and her elder sister (Mrs. Blessing) called me and said she was going to support me with part of the money to pay for their flight. It meant a lot to me because I had spent so much money then. I re-paid the flight, and they took off to Rwanda while I was there. I took two friends in Rwanda to accompany me to the airport to pick up my family. We waited at the airport for a long time, and there was no trace of my family. Everyone on that flight had been onboard the plane, but I did not see my family. I told my friends that we should wait again for thirty more minutes, and if they did not show up, I would make a complaint. I was losing my patience as time passed for years. I waited for years to reunite with my family, and every second was a test of patience and perpetually becoming painful for me.

Fifteen minutes later, I saw my two beautiful girls, and my daughter ran to me. The joy I felt holding my daughter for the first time was uncontrollable. My heart melted when I hugged her for the first time; it felt like my happiness was completed that day. I immersed myself in that moment; if I could stop the time, I would stop it at that moment. I cherished that moment to its fullest; she knew I was her dad, and she reciprocated the emotions just like me. In her eyes, I could see her love for me; she smiled, giggled, and was driven in with the utmost excitement. If I had to put that moment in a nutshell, I would say that every second apart melted away, leaving only the warmth of her presence.

As for my wife, at first glance at her, my heart was pounding very hard; I couldn't bear the anticipation of love and joy. After years of separation, we finally reunited; her presence brought a magical radiance, illuminating my life with exuberance. It felt like ahead of me stood a part of me that I had been seeking for all this time. When she was heading my way, it felt like all my happiness had just blossomed; the nearer she got to me, the more relieved I felt and the more ravishing she got in my eyes. The moment she hugged me and wrapped her arm around me, all my pain faded away, and all that was left was affection and adoration for her. On that day, upon seeing and hugging my wife, I wouldn't have envied the souls in heaven because I was in bliss myself.

My daughter had only seen me over video calls, but she ran straight to me, and that right there is what they say, "Blood is thicker than water." I took my girlfriend and our daughter to a restaurant that night, and we went home after. I did not sleep that night because I was only staring at my daughter, how she was sleeping so peacefully. I was thinking and saying to myself that this is my blood, and I had not even thought about being a father and having someone look up to me or depend on me. Even though I had processed all that before, meeting with my daughter in person changed everything.

After four years of not seeing each other, we had the best time ever. I decided to put a ring on my girlfriend's finger. We discussed it, and she agreed to marry me; we picked a date, did all the work, and we got married. All this happened in one month since I had only one month to be in Rwanda because of my job. Boom! The day of departure finally arrived, which was one of the worst days of my life.

On the departure, I saw my wife and daughter cry as if we were going to separate again. I could not control myself but shed tears and said goodbye. The separation from the love of my life and my child really had a mental toll on me; from the departure to the time I was on the plane, I was thinking about one thing: there could be a way I could have spent more time with my loved one. But there were responsibilities that I had to cater to.

I flew back to the States, and the same day I arrived, I lost my job on the same day. I said to myself, "Why did I not even stay longer?" You see how different situations change your perspective; just a few days before, I wished to spend more time with my family, and now I was somewhat regretting and wondering that I might have spent more time with my family, which eventually cost my job.

After losing my employment, things became so hard for me to get a job and to cater to my family. My wife has always supported me, and even though she does not work at all, she always understands the hardship I am going through. I enlisted in the military after six months of struggling as a Reservist. I was doing all this just to put papers for my family to move to the States so we could be together. I do not want to speak on some topics because of security purposes, but it is high time the immigration system in this country needs to be re-adjusted.

Today is July 26, 2024, and I still have not gotten the chance to bring my family over, which pains me so severely. I have put a lot of effort into bringing my family to the US. If you ask me, then I would say that providing your family money is one thing, and being close to them is another; the former is my obligation, and the latter is my goal. To this day, I would go the extra mile to have my family in the US, and I believe I can achieve this goal.

I finally graduated from boot camp, went to Tech school, completed Tech school, came out to the civilian world, and faced real hardship. I applied for jobs, did all kinds of training, and did all sorts of odd jobs to provide for my family, but things only got worse, making me avoid being there for my family. I am a very calm and shy person. I only get comfortable around people I know so much. I am more of a doer than a talker. So, if my wife says something to me, I might be quiet and work in the background to make it happen, but I will always get into problems with her because she thinks I am ignoring her. I thought she would have known that part of me by now, but no. I am trying so hard to change that part of me, but as we all know, change is a gradual process, and I am currently working on all my weaknesses. I was unemployed for seven months, and it could only be God who showed me ways to get money to pay my bills and still provide for my family. Things have not been the best between us. I know it is because she misses me and needs me to always be with her because, on a serious note, it is not easy to have a boyfriend when and you guys do not have time to spend together. Then you guys get married and still do not have time to spend quality time together, and this has been going on like this for the past seven years, but I keep praying God should intervene and bring us together so that we can make one happy family again.

Let us talk about my biggest surprise now. After my training, my cousin, who agreed to help me when I was coming to the States, started a class and told me that he could only assist me by teaching me and giving me the knowledge to get a job. There is a saying that "it is better to teach someone how to fish than to keep giving that person fish all the time," and that is what my cousin did. He taught me how to fish, and I was hungry, which let me learn fast and start fishing myself. I studied and studied and traveled to see him so that he could teach me more face-to-face. When I met with him and the family, they treated me well, and I felt loved by them; he opened up to me and told me what he was going through when I needed help, and I was speechless. That is why it is not good to judge someone until you are in their shoes. I came back with a different mindset and kept pushing and praying and asking God to intervene in my marriage because it was going out of control. Things are not the best now between me and my wife, but I know it will be better. My cousin gave me something that money could not buy, and that is "KNOWLEDGE." I used the knowledge to hunt for a job, and I got an interview and waited for three weeks to get a reply to no avail. I believe this phrase, "God's time is the best," is so because I got a reply on my birthday, which was on the 27th of June, and the response was as follows: "Hello, Harris! I have been given the approval to hire you. I am not in the office, but I will get you your offer letter tomorrow," That was the best birthday gift anyone could ever give me, and boom, the next day, they gave me my offer letter. Even though it was an out-of-state position, I give God all the glory because I needed some time to refresh my mind in a new and isolated area where no one knew me. In life, we might have Fifteen Thousand (15,000) square feet of houses, but we do not have a home, or we could have multiple cars, and we are not getting anywhere, or we could have nine hundred pairs of shoes, but we are not taking a step in the right direction. God gave me this job at the right time, and he put me in the right direction. A wise man once told me, "We might plan so hard for life, but life itself has a bigger plan for us." Two days after I received my offer letter to work in Space X, I got a promotion in the military. Tell me if my God is not worthy of my praise. There is no word to compare to what God has done for me in one week.

Who says God does not work in a mysterious way? After all this bundle of joy, HE gave me, it was time for me to start looking for accommodation in California. I had just five days to move to California and start work. So, I started looking for accommodation, and I found a house. The landlord told me that he had two rooms to rent, and he was going to give me one and the other room to a lady. The lady had made inquiries about it before I could contact him. The next day, this landlord called me to tell me that he would not give me the room again because the lady's parents refused because they did not want a man to live beside their daughter, and for that, they decided to pay for the two rooms. Now, I am screwed because I have just four more days left. I went back online and started hunting for accommodation, and God led me to another man. So, the mystery of this paragraph is that this man works in the same company that I am going to be working for. We agreed on everything. I drove for two days to California, and this man welcomed me with love and kindness. He is a veteran, and his wife and his kids are nice people. This is how when God says, "It is time for you to shine, you will shine." I have been finding favor in everything and everywhere I set my feet. I am doing very well in school, getting "A's" in all my courses, even though it is not easy handling school and work at the same time. This story is to encourage someone out there. No matter how hard life treats you or how difficult things seem to be, go down on your knees and pray without seizing; continue to hope for a better day because GOD's TIME IS THE BEST.

www.ingramcontent.com/pod-product-compliance
Lightning Source LLC
Chambersburg PA
CBHW051250120626
46547CB00014B/1877